KIDS DEVOTIONALS
Reading with Parents

"Then He went down with them and came to Nazareth, and was obedient to them, but His mother kept all these things in her heart. And Jesus increased in wisdom and stature, and in favor with God and men" (Luke 2: 51-52).

Nancy Petrey

I0225063

Energion Publications

Gonzalez, Florida

2023

Original Cover Art: Justin Jacobs (southluvernebc.com)

Art Credits: Unless otherwise indicated, images are licensed from Adobe Stock. Images on pages 31 & 37 are in the public domain. The image on page 46 is licensed from iStock. The image of the girl with suitcase on page 52 is licensed from Dreamstime.com, and the globe is downloaded from Pixabay.com.

ISBN: 978-1-63199-879-9
eISBN: 978-1-63199-880-5
Library of Congress Control Number: 2023947131

Eudokia Enrichment Library — An imprint of Energion Publications
1241 Conference Rd
Cantonment, FL 32533

pubs@energion.com
energion.com

DEDICATION

I dedicate this book to all my friends, including those on social media
and my email list of prayer warriors,
who have encouraged me and prayed for me,
as I was writing these devotionals.
Their positive comments on the devotionals
I posted on Facebook spurred me on
to complete this book.
There are too many to call names,
but I thank the Lord for their very real participation,
and I lift them up in prayer to the Father for blessings.

ACKNOWLEDGMENTS

First, I want to acknowledge and thank my publishers, Henry and Jody Neufeld of Energion Publications, for accepting this book for publication and placing it in their launch of home school resources for elementary school children. This will be the ninth book they have published for me. Working with them is always a good experience, and they do excellent work.

My reviewer and proofreader is my son, Jim Petrey. He began this service for me with my *Family Secrets Trilogy* two years ago. I really appreciate his time and viewpoint as a well-read adult. His help has been invaluable, and I am very grateful to him.

It has been a special blessing to me that my pastor, Justin Jacobs, provided the artistic rendering of his family photo – wife Andi and children, Harper and Carter – for the cover. The goal of this book shines forth in his picture. Justin took time out from his busy schedule as a pastor to do this, and I am so thankful.

Not finally, but foremost, I acknowledge the Holy Spirit who gave me the theme of each devotional, the Scripture selections, and the guidance to put it all together. He motivated me to write for children, and this is my first effort to do so. My brother Ben and his wife Valerie are about to "try it out" on their grandsons as part of their home schooling.

My prayer is that children will be inspired by the teaching and biblical examples in each devotional, and it will be a part of molding their young lives and keep them from having to learn things "the hard way." I also pray that parents will be sensitive to their children's needs and will not cut short the suggested prayers and questions at the end of each devotional. May their discussions be led by the Holy Spirit, and may both parents and children feel that it's not a duty, but a joy, to read together.

Table of Contents

NOTE TO PARENTS

Bringing up children in the society we are living in today is quite a challenging job. I pray this book will be helpful to parents as they seek to raise their children in the "nurture and admonition of the Lord" (Eph. 6:4). I began to write these devotionals because I saw the need for a book like this, but I did not have a specific call from the Lord to write it. However, as I continued to write, I was impressed that the Master Teacher was feeding me the subjects and the accompanying Scripture. I sensed how appropriate these Bible lessons are for young minds. Then the Lord began to reveal Himself to me and to affirm my writing, as several "God incidents" happened. These were not coincidences, but they were evidences of God's hand on me as I was inspired by the Holy Spirit.

Children, ages 8 to 11, or 3rd through 6th graders, are the ones for whom I wrote this. The devotionals are to be read by one or both parents to the child/children, or the child/children can read them with a parent present. Hopefully, discussion will ensue, and the spiritual lessons taught will help to solve problems, motivate right actions, and cause the child to be molded into the image of Jesus. Other byproducts could be drawing the parent and child into a closer relationship and increasing Bible knowledge.

Depending on the family's time schedule, some of the lessons might be too long or have too much information for one sitting, so these particular ones could be divided into two sections for two sittings. In fact several days could be allotted for certain devotionals that stir the interest of the child. The family needs to decide how to use this book in accordance with the time set apart for this spiritual experience. A Bible for the parents and a Bible for the child (same translation) is a necessary part of reading these devotionals.

May the Holy Spirit make His presence known,

Nancy Petrey

1. Only One Rule

"So God created Adam [human beings] in his own image. In the image of God he created them; male and female he created them. Then God blessed them and said, 'Be fruitful and multiply. Fill the earth and govern it. Reign over the fish in the sea, the birds in the sky, and all the animals that scurry along the ground'" (Genesis 1:26, NLT).

What did Adam and Eve do in the Garden of Eden that caused God to punish them? They disobeyed Him. He only gave them one rule, and they broke it! God had made a perfect and beautiful place for them to live with delicious food hanging from the trees or growing out of the ground. He created every kind of animal to play with. Adam even got to name each animal. None of them would bite or scratch or sting. Adam and Eve could use an elephant's trunk as a strong rope to swing them up to his back! They could make a giraffe bend his long neck down, so they could climb aboard and ride him. In fact all the animals obeyed them, no matter what they were commanded to do. Adam and Eve could run and play without giving out of breath or stubbing their toes. They could climb trees and not fall and swim all day long in beautiful rivers and lakes. They never got tired or sunburned. Their lives were exciting and fun every day. So why did they disobey God, and how did He punish them?

For disobeying Him, God sent them out of the garden. Besides all the other trees there were two special trees, the tree of life and the tree of the knowledge of good and evil in the middle of the garden. God said the fruit of one of them they should not eat. It was the tree of the knowledge of good and evil. Eating of it would cause them to die! They thought they really loved God, but His rule didn't make sense, and they ate the fruit. As soon as they did, they felt awful! Their consciences hurt them, and they tried to hide from God. He had been so good to them and had given them everything they wanted except for that one rule.

Adam and Eve disobeyed God, and now they wouldn't have this perfect Garden of Eden to live in anymore. They would have to work very hard to get enough food out of the ground to feed themselves. Outside the garden there were thorns, and the ground was as hard as rock. The animals wouldn't obey them anymore. They were afraid of Adam and Eve and would snarl and spit and claw if they got too close. Adam and Eve couldn't face God because now He knew they didn't really love Him, or they would have obeyed. Nothing would ever be the same again.

God's desire was for the man and woman He created to love Him because they wanted to, not because He forced them to. That's why God gave them that one rule. Their obedience would prove they really did love Him. But God was so merciful. He made a way for them to come back. They had sinned, and they were banished from His presence. The penalty for their sin was death. But God would later send Someone to die in their place, and He would save them from their sins and take them to Heaven, an even better place than the Garden of Eden! He would be their Savior. God would name Him – Jesus! He obeyed His Heavenly Father, as well as His earthly parents.

PRAYER: Dear God, thank You for all the things you give me, especially good food, my pet, the beautiful earth, and my parents who love me. Thank You for Jesus who forgives my sins and saves me. Help me obey You and to obey my parents.

QUESTIONS: What one rule did God give Adam and Eve? (Read Genesis 2:16-17.) Who did God send to die in my place? (Read Matthew 1:21.) What did Jesus say proved our love? (Read John 14:15.)

2. Honor and Obey

"Then He went down with them and came to Nazareth, and was obedient to them, but His mother kept all these things in her heart. And Jesus increased in wisdom and stature, and in favor with God and men" (Luke 2:51-52).

When Jesus was twelve years old, He went with his parents, Mary and Joseph, from their home in Nazareth to Jerusalem, God's Holy City. This city was the one God picked for His chosen people, the Jews, to travel to from all over Israel three times a year to make animal sacrifices. The place for the sacrifices was at His Temple.

The people were celebrating the Feast of Passover, remembering the time two thousand years ago when God brought their ancestors out of Egypt where they had been slaves to the Pharaoh for 400 years. They had been whipped and beaten, building for Pharaoh! God had told them He was going to punish Pharaoh and the Egyptians with plagues so they would let the Israelites leave Egypt. The plagues would not hurt them if they would do one thing. They had to kill a perfect lamb and spread his blood on the doorposts of their houses. When he saw the blood, the death angel would pass over their houses, but he would enter the houses of the Egyptians and kill their first-born sons, even Pharaoh's. The first plague was their Nile River turning to blood. Then came frogs, lice, flies, disease on the livestock, boils, hail, locusts, and darkness. These plagues covered the land of Egypt! Death of the first-born sons and first-born of the animals was the tenth plague. Pharaoh finally let the Jews leave.

The boy Jesus had so many questions about this Passover feast. He knew He was the Son of God, the Firstborn, because His mother had told Him. She wouldn't answer His questions about the meaning of that, so as soon as they got to Jerusalem, He headed straight for the temple.

He found some teachers sitting around and teaching people about the Scripture and the meaning of Passover. He got up close, listened intently and then began asking them questions. The teachers were amazed at what the boy already knew. They probably began asking HIM questions! One teacher took Him to his house and gave Him food and a place to sleep. (What Jesus did those days at the temple is not in the Bible, but it could have happened like this. The whole story is in Luke 2:41-52.)

Three days had passed before He realized His parents must be worried about Him. At that moment His mother came in the temple and saw Him! Mary said, "Son, why have You done this to us? We were traveling home and realized you weren't with us! Now we have come back, and Your father and I have been looking for you everywhere!" Jesus said to them, "Why did you look for Me? Didn't you know I had to be about My Father's business?" Jesus knew for certain now that God was His Father.

Joseph probably reminded Jesus that God commanded children to honor their parents and to obey them. Jesus knew He was the Son of God, but He was also the son of Mary and Joseph. He went back to Nazareth with them and was obedient to them. This pleased God and made Him wise and loved.

PRAYER: Dear Father in heaven, please help me to obey my parents no matter how I feel. I don't want to disobey and be punished like Adam and Eve. Thank You for showing me that by obeying my parents, I am also obeying You, and my conscience won't hurt me.

QUESTIONS: (First read Deut. 5:16 and Ephesians 6:1-3.) What two things did God promise children if they would honor and obey their parents? How can you honor them? What does honor mean?

3. Thanks and Praise

"Enter into His gates with thanksgiving, and into His courts with praise. Be thankful unto Him and bless His name. For the Lord is good; His mercy is everlasting, and His truth endures to all generations" (Psalm 100:4-5).

You may have seen the movie, "The Ten Commandments," the Bible story about the Israelites in slavery in Egypt and God sending Moses to lead them out. There may have been as many as three million Israelites escaping from the cruel Pharaoh and walking through the Red Sea, while the Egyptians in chariots on horses were chasing them. God blew the waters back and made a dry path to walk on with walls of water on each side. His people got across. The Egyptians followed them, and then God caused the water to crash down on the Egyptian soldiers, and they were drowned! It's wonderful that a movie was made of this true story. It helps us realize God's awesome miracle power in saving His people.

Did God's people thank Him? Yes, they did! Moses created a song to describe this miraculous deliverance, and his sister Miriam led the people in the song, with the women joining her in dancing with their tambourines. *"I will sing to the Lord, for He has triumphed gloriously! The horse and its rider He has thrown into the sea! The Lord is my strength and song, and He has become my salvation; He is my God, and I will praise Him; my father's God, and I will exalt Him" (Exodus 15:1,2,20,21).*

If someone saved your life, you would thank that person with all your heart and try to show him how much you appreciate what he did for you. You probably would wrap your arms around him and hug him as tight as you could. You would keep thanking him with words, and you might buy him a gift. You would tell others about his greatness. Moses showed his thankful heart by creating a song about their salvation. Miriam showed her gratitude by leading others to sing and dance with her.

Jesus taught the importance of a thankful heart in His story about the ten lepers (Luke 17:11-19). They all asked for healing, and all were healed, but only one thanked Jesus. This man and the others had gone to show the priests that they were healed, but only one came back. The leper with the thankful heart gave glory to God with a loud voice, fell down on his face at Jesus' feet and gave Him thanks. He was a Samaritan, not one of God's chosen people. He put to shame the other nine men who were so selfish they wouldn't take the time to return to Jesus and thank him that their fingers, toes, and noses were no longer eaten away. Now they could go back to their homes and be in public because their contagious disease of leprosy was gone! They were clean!

Psalm 100 tells us "The Lord is good; His mercy is everlasting, and His truth endures to all generations." God wants us to come close to Him. "Enter into His **gates** with thanksgiving, and into His **courts** with praise. Be thankful unto Him and bless His name." One day Jesus will be King over the whole world, including us. We won't be able to get close to him unless we come through the **gate** of the temple into His throne room with **thanksgiving**. And if we want to get really close to our King, we have to enter His **courts** with **praise**. Moses exalted Him by singing praises of His greatness.

PRAYER: Dear Jesus, I do thank you. I know I don't say it enough. Sometimes I keep my mouth closed when they are singing in church. Help me to count my blessings like the song says that we sing at Thanksgiving time. Help me get over being embarrassed to show my love for you. Thank You!

QUESTION: Do you ever say thank you to your parents for giving you food, clothes, a home, fun gifts and trips, and maybe even a pet? Do you exalt (brag on) them with compliments? Make a response to their love.

4. Substitute

*"Then Abraham lifted his eyes and looked, and there behind him was a ram caught in a thicket by its horns. So Abraham went and took the ram and offered it up for a burnt offering **instead** of his son (Genesis 22:13).*

Sometimes your school teacher has to be absent. It may be that she is sick or has an appointment with the dentist, or there's some other reason. But you will still have your class. The principal will call for a substitute. This substitute teacher may not be as good as your real teacher, but she takes the place of your real teacher that day. The meaning of the word "substitute" is "takes the place of."

When Adam and Eve disobeyed God and ate of the tree of the knowledge of good and evil, God said they would die. They didn't die immediately, but they would grow old and die one day. They were no longer close to God and had to live outside the Garden of Eden. They lived hundreds of years, working hard for their food, clothing, and shelter. God gave them a good start outside the garden by making clothes for them out of animal skins.

God had to kill an animal to do this. The poor animal had to die for Adam and Eve's sin! They didn't get away with disobeying God. Somebody had to die in their place. The animal was their SUBSTITUTE. This was the first animal sacrifice. God taught Cain and Abel, the children of Adam and Eve, about the need for sacrifices. When someone sinned, he would die, unless a sacrifice was made, and an animal took the place of the sinner.

When the boy Jesus and His parents went to Jerusalem at Passover to make a sacrifice, they took a firstborn lamb from their flock of sheep four days before the sacrifice. Jesus got to play with it for four days, and He was heartbroken that His pet lamb was going to be killed. Also there would be a perfect lamb sacrificed for the whole nation of Israel. He couldn't help but cry. It hurt Him to think that His father Joseph would have to cut the throat of His pet lamb, so their family would be forgiven for their sins by the lamb being their substitute. He just had to understand it better, and He knew the teachers at the temple could explain why God required this. Time passed so quickly that He missed the caravan of His parents traveling back to Nazareth. The teachers taught about the first Passover lamb when the Israelites, their ancestors, were told by Moses to kill their lamb and spread its blood on the doorposts and lintel (top of the doorway), get inside the house, and eat the roasted lamb. The death angel would PASS OVER every house that had the lamb's blood on it, and everyone in the house would be saved from death. But the Egyptians' firstborn sons would die. Then the Pharaoh would finally let the Israelites leave Egypt and their life of slavery.

The boy Jesus remembered that He was the firstborn of His parents, and He also remembered the Scripture about Abraham being told by God to sacrifice His beloved only son Isaac (Genesis 22). It upset Him until the priest reminded Him about the big sheep (ram) caught by his horns in the thorn bush near them. God stopped Abraham from killing Isaac and said the ram was to be his substitute.

PRAYER: Dear Father, help me realize how serious it is to sin. Someone has to die in my place, so I don't have to die. Thank You, Jesus. I know Your name means "God saves." You died in my place like the sheep died in Isaac's place. Thank You for saving me from my sins.

QUESTION: What promise did God make to Abraham? (Read Genesis 22:15-18.)

…d Abraham said ..*My Son . . God will provide himself a lamb for a burnt-offering*

JB

5. Messiah

"For unto us a Child is born, unto us a Son is given; and the government will be upon His shoulder. And His name will be called Wonderful, Counselor, Mighty God, Everlasting Father, Prince of Peace" (Isaiah 9:6).

God called Isaiah to be a **prophet** to the Jewish people and to speak about the future to them and to the king of Judah, King Ahaz, who was so afraid of the King of Assyria and his threats to destroy Israel and Judah. Isaiah said that a Son was going to be born in Judah to a young unmarried woman (Isaiah 7:14), and they would call Him **Immanuel**. In the Hebrew language that name meant "God with us." Isn't that amazing? This little boy would be God and would live with them! How could that happen? Then Isaiah said He would rule their government! They didn't have to be afraid of the King of Assyria. These are Isaiah's words from God to them: *"For unto us a Child is born, unto us a Son is given; and the government will be upon His shoulder. And His name will be called Wonderful, Counselor, Mighty God, Everlasting Father, Prince of Peace" (Isaiah 9:6).* How could a child be their ruler, their king?

You know the name Jesus Christ. It is a Greek name. Jesus the Messiah is a Hebrew name. Both mean the same thing, "Anointed One." When the Hebrews crowned a new king, he would be anointed, meaning they would pour oil on his head. The oil meant the Holy Spirit was giving him power to rule over the people. Remember that the angel told Joseph to name his and Mary's baby, Jesus. The Hebrew name Yeshua actually means "God saves." The baby was given that name because He would SAVE His people from their sins. He would be the Christ, the Messiah! He would be the substitute sacrifice, **dying for our sins, not His**.

This baby that Isaiah was telling them about wasn't born until 700 years later. He was born and was placed in an animal feeding trough, a manger, and He didn't have a throne or a palace, but He would one day become King. Remember when the wise men, who were kings from the east, bowed down and worshiped the child Jesus and gave Him gold? They knew it was a gift fit for a king! But Jesus never became King of Israel. Instead, He was crucified on a cross by Roman soldiers. He died. They buried Him. But three days later He came back alive. For 40 days He taught His disciples, and then He rose up in the air and went back to His heavenly Father. Two angels told the people looking up and watching Him rise on clouds that Jesus would come back to earth the same way they saw Him go up.

So, it wasn't time for Jesus to rule the earth. He would come back when it was time, and after many people had come to believe in Him. His disciples would go out and tell the good news that His sacrifice on the cross brought forgiveness to all people and eternal life in heaven. Jesus had died as their substitute, and they were saved from their sins. All they had to do was believe in Him and accept His sacrifice. He was the Lamb of God who took away their sins at His FIRST coming. Now they could look forward to His SECOND coming when He would sit on His throne in Jerusalem as King over all the earth. He was the Messiah that all God's prophets said was coming. They had always looked for Him! God wants us to look for Him, too.

PRAYER: Oh Father, there is so much evil in the world today. Only the Messiah, the Prince of Peace, can fix everything that is wrong. Please send Him back to us soon to rule the world. Help me to tell my friends and family that He is coming, and we should be ready. We should ask Him to save us.

FILL IN BLANKS: Isaiah was one of God's _____. He told the people things that would happen in the _____.

6. Children at the Cross

"Then they [Roman soldiers] compelled a certain man, Simon a Cyrenian, the father of Alexander and Rufus, as he was coming out of the country and passing by, to bear His cross" (Mark 15:21).

John the Baptist and Jesus were cousins. John was a prophet. One day he was baptizing people in the Jordan River and looked up and saw Jesus coming toward him. He said, "Behold! The Lamb of God who takes away the sin of the world" (John 1:29). What did John mean? The day was coming when it would actually happen. It would be on Passover.

Jesus had been arrested. He was taken to court, and the Jewish leaders led by the High Priest said because He claimed to be God, He should be crucified! The Roman soldiers beat Him with a cruel whip. They laughed at Him and spit on Him. Then they made a crown of thorns and pressed it down on His head. He was bloody and so weak He could hardly carry the large crossbeam on his back. He kept falling down under its weight.

Jews from all over the land had come to Jerusalem to celebrate the Passover and make their sacrifice at the temple. Each family brought a lamb. And there was a lamb sacrificed for the whole nation also. People were lining the street called the Via Dolorosa (Way of Suffering) and saw Jesus being taken up the hill to Golgotha (Place of the Skull) where the Romans crucified people. Among the crowd was a man from Cyrene, a place in north Africa. It was Simon, and he had brought his two sons, Alexander and Rufus, with him to celebrate the Passover. The soldiers chose him from the crowd to help Jesus carry His cross.

There is a beautiful song, written and sung by Ray Bolz, describing what Simon and his children saw and felt. They watched the whole crucifixion. Ray Bolz made up the story, but it is likely close to the truth. The name of one of these boys, Rufus, appears in Scripture later (Rom. 16:13), and he was a part of the first church. What he saw that day showed him that Jesus really was the Lamb of God who took away the sins of the world. More than that, Rufus learned later that He rose from the dead, went back up into heaven, and will be coming back to earth someday to really be the King of the Jews. That title was written on His cross, but He will also be King of the World! Listen to the song, "Watch the Lamb."

https://youtu.be/UNT1AThOgME

Here are a few of the words:
"Walking on the road to Jerusalem,
the time had come to sacrifice again.
My two small sons,
they walked beside me down the road.
The reason that they came was to watch the lamb....

I told them of Moses, and Father Abraham,
and I said, 'Dear children, Watch the Lamb....

There will be so many in Jerusalem today,
we must be sure this little lamb doesn't run away,' ....

Then someone said, 'There's Jesus.'
I scarce believed my eyes,
a man so badly beaten,
He barely looked alive....

I watched Him when He fell.

The cross came down upon His back,
and the crowd began to yell...

the Roman soldier grabbed my arm and screamed,
 'YOU! CARRY HIS CROSS!'....

They led us to Golgotha.
They drove nails,
deep in His feet and hands,
and on the cross I heard him pray,
'Father, forgive them"....

'Into thy hands I commit my spirit,' He prayed,
and then He died....

My children stood there weeping,
and I heard the oldest say,
'Father please forgive us,
the lamb, ran away...

I took them in my arms,
we turned and faced the cross,
and I said, 'Dear children, WATCH THE LAMB...'

Read the complete lyrics:

https://lyrics.lyricfind.com/lyrics/ray-boltz-watch-the-lamb

PRAYER: Thank You, Father, that You so loved the world that You gave Your only begotten Son, that whoever believes in Him will not die but have everlasting life! I believe in Jesus!! I love Him for being the Lamb of God who took away my sin.

FILL IN THE BLANKS: (Read Matt. 1:20-21.) Joseph was told by an _____of the____ in a _____to name his and Mary's baby _____ (Yeshua in Hebrew) for He will _____ His people from their _____.

7. Parents Know Best

"As an eagle stirs up its nest, hovers over its young, spreading out his wings, taking them up, carrying them on its wings, so the Lord alone led him [Israel], and there was no foreign god with him [walking in the desert to the promised land]" (Deut. 32:11-12).

It is interesting that Simon the Cyrenian was identified as the father of Alexander and Rufus in only the Gospel of Mark, but Matthew and Luke do record that he took Jesus' cross and carried it for Him. Every word in the Bible was put there by the Holy Spirit of God, so there is a reason that it is written that Simon had his two sons with him on that feast day of Passover. For some reason God wanted us to even know their names. We get the idea that Simon must have been a good father. It's possible he was training his boys to do the right thing, taking them with him to Jerusalem. It is also possible that they didn't want to go and their father had to almost push them out the door to make the journey, just as God had commanded it. *"Three times a year all your males shall appear before the* Lord *your God in the place which He chooses: at the Feast of Unleavened Bread, at the Feast of Weeks, and at the Feast of Tabernacles; and they shall not appear before the* Lord *empty-handed" (Deut. 16:16).* They had a lamb with them to sacrifice.

Here is a funny poem, showing how a parent might have to teach his child to obey the Lord's commands, whether he likes it or not. The mother eagle has to actually push her little eaglets out of the nest, or they will never learn to fly and escape their enemy who would like to have them for lunch! If parents let children have their own way instead of making them do the right thing, they are hurting their children. Children have to learn that their parents know best, whatever it feels like.

BILLY BOB, THE EAGLET

Hey, little eaglet, up there soaring in the sky,
Tell about the time when you thought that you would die.
Billy Bob answered and began to tell his tale:
"It all started one day when Mama had a spell!
"Her eyes were full of fire, and she hopped into the nest;
"She pulled the downy feathers out! Us eaglets had no rest.
"Before she started going mad, we were comfy as could be,
"But now the nest was sticky – oh, it hurt! Couldn't she see?
"Mama fixed her gaze on me and shoved me to the edge!
"Stop it, Mama! I'll fall off and hit the rocky ledge!"
"But she paid no attention to all my fearful cries,
"And then I started falling, and the ground began to rise!
"I prayed for God to save me; then I heard a loud smack!
"Mama had swooped down, and she caught me on her back!
"She flew me high above the clouds. I finally caught my breath.
"I never felt so free, and soon I lost my fear of death.
"She gently placed me in the nest and told me I must rest.
"I guess she thought her Billy Bob had passed this horrible test!
"But when the next day dawned, Mama did the same again,
"And she said, 'Fly! You've got wings! I know that you can!'
"So I did my best to flap and fly, but all to no avail,
"And Mama caught me once again and said, 'All is well.'
"You see, I finally learned that my Mama I could trust.
"Now I love soaring in the sky, and I've never bitten the dust!"
(Ex. 19:4; Deut. 32:11; Psalm 103:5; Isa. 40:31)
By Nancy Petrey ~ July 16, 2019

PRAYER: Dear heavenly Father, I know I can trust You, and You have given me parents I can trust, even when they don't give me what I want. They know much more than I do, and they are only making me obey them for my own good. Help me not to be mean to them. In Jesus' name. Amen.

QUESTIONS: What clue is in the Bible that makes us think that Simon of Cyrene was a good father? (Read Romans 16:13.) What promise does God make to parents about raising up their children? (Read Proverbs 22:6.)

8. Listen

"Come, my children, and __listen__ to me, and I will teach you to fear the Lord. Does anyone want to live a life that is long and prosperous? Then keep your tongue from speaking evil and your lips from telling lies! Turn away from evil and do good. Search for peace, and work to maintain it" (Psalms 34:11-14, NLT).

Somebody said that we have two ears and only one mouth because God wants us to listen twice as much as He wants us to speak. What we listen to will later come out of our mouths, whether good or bad. God is saying to you, "Come, My children, and listen to Me..." If you want a long, happy life, watch what you say. Don't lie. Respect the Lord. Turn your back on acting bad, and do good things for people. Be a peacemaker when you are with your friends and your brothers and sisters and cousins. Don't argue and fuss with them.

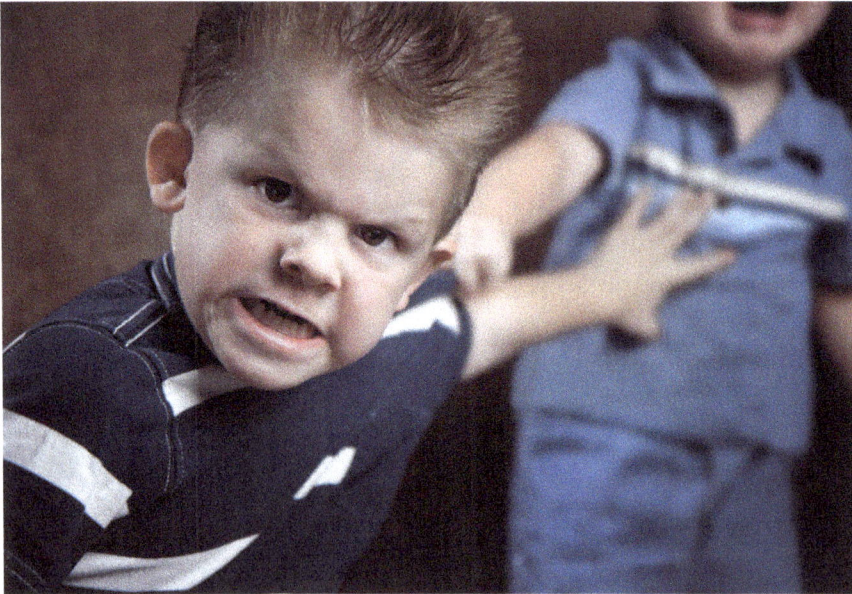

If you want to please God, listen to what He says. Believe Him. Have faith in Him. This is what God told His servant Paul to teach the church people at Rome and everywhere. He said, "And it is impossible to please God without faith. Anyone who wants to come to Him must believe that God exists and that He rewards those who sincerely seek Him" (Hebrews 11:6, NLT).

How do you get faith? "So then faith comes by **hearing**, and hearing by the Word of God" (Rom. 10:17). If you want to be rewarded, **listen** to your preacher and your Sunday school teacher, as well as your parents, when they are reading and explaining the Bible to you. Even better, **you** can read it out loud, and your two ears will hear it. It is like a seed planted in your heart that will grow and cause you to have a long and happy life!

Do you know how powerful the words of God are? He spoke, and the world was created! He said, "Let there be light!" And there **was** light! Jesus said, "The words that I speak to you are spirit, and they are life" (John 6:63). His words have power when you speak them out loud!

James, the brother of Jesus, wrote one of the books of the Bible. He said, "Understand this, my dear brothers and sisters: You must all be **quick to listen,** slow to speak, and slow to get angry. Human anger does not produce the righteousness God desires." (James 1:19-20, NIV).

There was another James who followed Jesus. He and his brother John were sons of Zebedee, and they were hotheads. Once when Jesus was traveling through Samaria on the way to Jerusalem, He was refused lodging because the Samaritans didn't like Jews. James and John wanted to call down fire from heaven and destroy them! Jesus was very upset with them and rebuked them (Luke 9:51-58). He knew How temperamental they were and had already nicknamed them "Sons of Thunder." If the brothers had been listening to Jesus say that we must love our enemies, they might have held their tongues. Being around Jesus did finally change them, so they could be "quick to listen, slow to speak, and slow to get angry." They learned how to listen to the Holy Spirit when they got upset. The Spirit caused them to remember things Jesus had said that kept them from feeling anger. They waited to speak. Temperamental John changed to "the Apostle of Love."

PRAYER: Dear Father in heaven, help me to be quick to listen, slow to speak, and slow to get angry. Show me how important and powerful the words of Jesus are. I want to be rewarded with a long and happy life. Make my faith grow, Lord, by hearing your Word spoken and by speaking it out loud myself, so I can enjoy my life and stay healthy in my mind and body. Amen.

QUESTIONS: When you start to get angry, what must you do first? Who is it you need to listen to at that moment?

9. The Greatest

"Then a dispute arose among them as to which of them would be greatest. And Jesus, perceiving the thought of their heart, took a little child and set him by Him, and said to them, 'Whoever receives this little child in My name receives Me; and whoever receives Me receives Him who sent Me. For he who is least among you all will be great'" (Luke 9:46-48).

The first king of Israel was Saul, but God removed him from being king because he didn't obey the Lord. Then God sent His prophet Samuel to pick out a king for Israel who would obey Him. Samuel went to the house of Jesse, who had eight sons. Samuel looked at the first one and thought this son would be the king God was looking for because he was very tall and looked like a king. But God told Samuel, "... the Lord does not see as man sees; for man looks at the outward appearance, but the Lord looks at the heart" (1 Samuel 16: 7). Jesse didn't think his youngest son David would be considered, so he didn't even show him to Samuel. When Samuel asked if he had any more sons, Jesse had to go outside and get David. He was watching over the sheep. The minute Samuel saw him, he said, "This is the one!" Samuel anointed David with oil, and the Holy Spirit came on him, giving him power to be King one day. Saul was tall and handsome and looked like a king, and David seemed unimportant. He was only a shepherd boy, but he became known as "a man after God's own heart." (Story from 1 Samuel 16:1-13.)

Jesus had to teach His disciples to be more like children if they wanted to be great. He said, "Unless you change and become like little children, you will by no means enter the kingdom of heaven" (Matt. 18:3). Think about it, why did Jesus use a little child as an example of greatness and an example of a person worthy of being in His kingdom? One thing a little child doesn't have is pride. God hates pride. A child knows he is small and doesn't understand much. A child usually has a trusting heart and believes what you tell him. He can be easily molded into the kind of person Jesus wants to represent Him. A "know-it-all" teenager or adult won't listen to instruction. A little child has a mind like a sponge and is thirsty to soak up all you tell him. He will be a loyal follower, and he will be eager to tell others what he has been taught. A little child receives love easily and shares that love with everyone equally. He doesn't think he is better than others. That's probably why Jesus chose a small child as an example of greatness.

PRAYER: Dear Lord, please help me not to be a "know-it-all" or a "show-off." Help me to realize that Jesus already gave children an advantage over older people who have more knowledge than they do. Don't let me lose my trusting nature. Help me to enjoy being what God made me as a child – carefree, eager to learn and eager to go tell what I am taught. Thank You, Jesus, for calling me "great."

QUESTIONS: What kind of argument were Jesus' disciples having when He brought a little child to them? (Read Luke 9:46-48.) Why did David, a young shepherd boy without weapons, think he could defeat Goliath, the Philistine giant, who was threatening to destroy the army of Israel? Who was he depending on? (Read 1 Samuel 16:1-13.)

10. Weakest and Youngest

Gideon was scared to death when he heard the Midianites were coming to steal the crops of the Israelites. He hid in the winepress to thresh his wheat. *"And the Angel of the* Lord *appeared to him, and said to him, 'The* Lord *is with you, YOU MIGHTY MAN OF VALOR [courage]!'....Then the* Lord *turned to him and said, 'Go in this might of yours, and you shall save Israel from the hand of the Midianites. Have I not sent you? So he said to Him, 'O my Lord, how can I save Israel? Indeed my clan is the **weakest** in Manasseh, and I am the **least** in my father's house.' And the* Lord *said to him, 'Surely **I will be with you**, and you shall defeat the Midianites as one man'"* (Judges 6:12-16).

Most people would have called Gideon a coward, but God called him a mighty warrior! God sees people for what they **will become** with His help. But why would God choose Gideon to lead the army of Israel to victory over the Midianites, whose troops greatly outnumbered Israel, when his clan was the weakest in his tribe, and he was the least in his family? If you read the story in the Book of Judges you will find out that God's battle plan was unbelievable! He wanted the army trimmed down to only 300 men, but the Midianites and their camels couldn't even be counted they were so many! The weapons God chose were ridiculous! Each man held a trumpet, an empty pitcher, and a torch. God chose their loud voices as weapons also. Gideon divided his army into three companies, and they encircled the camp of the Midianites who were fast asleep. Gideon told his men to watch him and do what he did. He put his pitcher over his torch in his left hand. He held a trumpet in his right hand. Gideon blew the trumpet and broke the pitcher, so the torch would blaze forth. Then he shouted, "The sword of the Lord and of Gideon!" All his men did the same, and the Midianites were jolted wide awake and thought a huge army was about to destroy them. They were filled with fear! The Lord made them turn on each other and fight against themselves! Then they ran. Gideon's army, joined by men from all over Israel, ran after the Midianites and defeated them. (Judges 7:16-22).

God chose Gideon, knowing he would carry out His battle plan, no matter how strange it was. The size of Gideon's army was only 300 because God had sent thousands of the volunteers home and had left only a small number. Here's why: "And the Lord said to Gideon, 'The people who are with you are too many for Me to give the Midianites into their hands, **lest Israel claim glory for itself against Me, saying, 'My own hand has saved me'**" (Judges 7:2). God wants the glory when He performs His miracles. There are many times in the Bible that God chose the ones you would least expect through whom to show His power. He would use the weakest and the youngest, the ones who would give God the credit. They would know it wasn't their own power. Paul taught the church at Corinth: "God chose things the world considers foolish in order to shame those who think they are wise. And he chose things that are powerless to shame those who are powerful. God chose things despised by the world, things counted as nothing at all, and used them to bring to nothing what the world considers important. As a result, no one can ever boast in the presence of God" (1 Corinthians 1:27-29, NLT).

PRAYER: Dear mighty God, thank You for using weak people and young people through whom to show Your power and wisdom. I am only a child, but You think I am important. Help me never to brag on myself but to brag on You, when You do great things through me. I want to be Your servant, Lord.

QUESTIONS: Why did God want Gideon to have an army of only 300 men? What was God's battle plan to defeat the Midianites, and what weapons did God choose?

11. Size Doesn't Matter

"We can't go up against them! They are stronger than we are!" So they spread this bad report about the land among the Israelites: "The land we traveled through and explored will devour anyone who goes to live there. All the people we saw were huge. We even saw giants there, the descendants of Anak. Next to them we felt like grasshoppers, and that's what they thought, too!" (Numbers 13:31-33, NLT).

God had promised His people, the Israelites, that He would take them out of Egypt. He would set them free from 400 years of slavery and take them to a land He had ready for them, the Promised Land of Canaan. They would cross the Red Sea, go through the desert, get the Law at Mt. Sinai, and then cross the Jordan River into the Promised Land. Moses was the man He prepared to lead them. When they arrived at the border of the Promised Land, Moses sent 12 men ahead to spy out the land, to see what it was like, what the people were like, if the towns had walls, and what kind of crops they were growing. (You can read this whole story in the Book of Numbers, Chapters 13 and 14.)

The spies explored the land for 40 days. They came back with a sample of the fruit they saw. They had cut down a branch with a single cluster of grapes so large that it took two of them to carry it on a pole between them! They said it was a bountiful country—a land flowing with milk and honey.... But the people living there were powerful, and their towns were large and fortified. They even saw giants there! The more the spies talked, the more afraid the people became. "But Caleb tried to quiet the people as they stood before Moses. 'Let's go at once to take the land,' he said. 'We can certainly conquer it!'" (Numbers 13:30, NLT). All 12 spies were leaders in Israel, but there were only two spies who believed God when He said He had given the land to them and commanded them to go in and defeat the Canaanites! Those two men were Caleb and Joshua.

(After Moses died 40 years later, Joshua would be the one to take them into the Promised Land.)

The people cried all night, and God was very angry at their disobedience and not believing that He was giving them the Land. Joshua and Caleb said to the Israelites, "Do not rebel against the Lord, and don't be afraid of the people of the land. They are only helpless prey to us! They have no protection, but the Lord is with us! Don't be afraid of them!" (Numbers 14:8-9). Joshua and Caleb had faith in God, that He would do what He said. The rest of the people didn't believe God. "Without faith, it is impossible to please God" (Heb. 11:6). So the Lord had to sentence the people to a life of wandering in the desert for 40 long years until all those unbelieving Israelites died out. Their children would follow Joshua into the Promised Land, and God would give them power to defeat the Canaanites, just like He said!

Think about it. Those disobedient people had seen God do miracles for them, and they still didn't believe Him. They saw the ten plagues that God sent on the Egyptians. They saw Him part the Red Sea so they could walk across on dry land, and they saw the Egyptian soldiers who came after them drown when God let the waters roll back! They saw God send them manna from heaven for their food. They saw a pillar of cloud lead them as they made camps in the desert. They saw a pillar of fire stay right over their camps at night to warm them. They saw Moses go up Mt. Sinai to get the Ten Commandments that God's finger wrote on stone tablets! Wouldn't you have believed God after seeing His power to provide for them and protect them in the desert? It didn't matter if there were giants in the Land, and the Israelites looked like grasshoppers compared to them! It didn't matter if the Egyptian army that came after them was bigger and more powerful than they were. Their God was bigger and more powerful than all the armies of the world, and He was on their side! Disobedience and lack of faith caused them to never see the Promised Land. Only Joshua and Caleb and the children of the disobedient Israelites went in!

PRAYER: Dear God, thank You that size doesn't matter. Although I am not full-grown, when I believe You want me to do something for You, I plan to do it! With Jesus' power, amen.

QUESTIONS: How angry did God get with the Israelites for not obeying Him and not going into Canaan and conquering it? (Read Numbers 14:10-12, 34.) What did Moses say about it? (Read Numbers 14:15-16, 19). Did the Lord listen to Moses? (Read Numbers 14:20-23.)

12. The Boy Samuel

"But Samuel ministered before the Lord, even as a child, wearing a linen ephod.... And the child Samuel grew in stature, and in favor both with the Lord and men" (1 Samuel 2:18, 26).

Samuel's mother Hannah had been unable to have a baby. She was teased all the time because the people believed that barrenness was a curse, that something about her displeased God. Everyone knew that children were gifts from the Lord, and she didn't have a child. Every year the people of Israel went to Shiloh, where the Ark of the Covenant was, to make their animal sacrifices. One year Hannah went to the Tabernacle at Shiloh (this was before the Temple was built in Jerusalem) to Eli the priest. It was there she prayed that God would give her a child. God answered, and Samuel was born. Hannah had promised she would give him to the Lord, so when he was around three years old, she went to Shiloh with her family and gave Samuel to Eli the priest to bring up as a minister to the Lord. She sewed a linen ephod, a colorful garment like a vest, for him to wear as a priest in the Tabernacle.

Eli had two wicked sons, Hophni and Phinehas, who served as priests with their father. They took the animal sacrifices, and the best ones for roasting they kept for themselves and badly treated the people. They also took some of the women for their own pleasure. Eli knew what they were doing, but he did nothing about their wicked behavior. All he did was tell them it wasn't right. He said, *"If one man sins against another, God will judge him. But if a man sins against the* Lord, *who will intercede [pray] for him?" (1 Samuel 2:25).* In other words, how could he ask God to forgive his wicked sons?

One day a man of God came to Eli and warned him, saying, *"Why do you kick at My sacrifice and My offering which I have commanded in My dwell-*

*ing place, and honor your sons more than Me, to make yourselves fat with the best of all the offerings of Israel My people?.... Now this shall be a sign to you that will come upon your two sons, on Hophni and Phinehas: **in one day they shall die**, both of them. Then I will raise up for Myself **a faithful priest** who shall do according to what is in My heart and in My mind. I will build him a sure house [descendants], and he shall walk before My anointed [King David] forever"* (1 Samuel 2:29, 34-35).

Who do you think became the "faithful priest"? Yes, you guessed right, the little boy Samuel. He was also God's **prophet**. [A priest speaks to God for the people. A prophet speaks to the people for God.] In those days God wasn't speaking to anyone because the people were wicked. But God chose to speak to Samuel after he lay down in his bed one night. The boy didn't recognize His voice. He thought it was Eli calling, and he went to see what he wanted. It happened three times. On the third time, Eli finally knew it was the Lord calling Samuel, and he told the boy to lie down and how to answer God. *"Now the* Lord *came and stood and called as at other times, 'Samuel! Samuel!' And Samuel answered, 'Speak, for Your servant **hears**.'"* (1 Samuel 3:10). It's interesting that Hannah named him Samuel, which means, "**heard** by God," because God heard and answered her prayer for a child.

The next morning Eli wanted to know what God said to Samuel. The boy was afraid to tell him such bad news, but he told him everything the Lord said. God could trust His boy **prophet** Samuel because he obeyed Him and spoke the truth. *"So Samuel grew, and the* Lord *was with him and let none of his words fall to the ground"* (1 Samuel 3:19). That meant that all the messages Samuel gave the people from the Lord would come true. Yes, Hophni and Phinehas were killed in battle with the Philistines, and the Ark of the Covenant was taken. It was a sad day in Israel. Do you see that God takes sin very seriously? But God had prepared ahead by using his boy prophet to begin building the nation of Israel back up. God was merciful, and Samuel helped to turn the heart of the people back to God.

PRAYER: Dear Lord, I want to be quick to hear You when you call me. Help me recognize Your voice and obey you even when it is very hard. Thank You for trusting a child with your messages. And Father, I am grateful to have parents who discipline me when I am bad. When I have children, please help me to discipline them so they won't turn out bad like Eli's sons did.

QUESTIONS: Do you think Hannah had heard about the wicked behavior of Eli's sons? Why would she leave her three-year-old son at the Tabernacle to be brought up by Eli? If you were Samuel, how would you feel to have to tell Eli what was going to happen to his sons and his descendants? What happened to Eli when he heard the news about his sons being killed in battle? (Read 1 Samuel 4:15-18.)

13. Jesus Loves Babies

*"Then they also brought **infants** to Him that He might touch them; but when the disciples saw it, they rebuked them. But Jesus called them to Him and said, 'Let the little children come to Me, and do not forbid them; for of such is the kingdom of God. Assuredly, I say to you, whoever does not receive the kingdom of God as a little child will by no means enter it" (Luke 18:15-17).*

Jesus was a patient teacher. His disciples were still thinking like the world does, not respecting the small, the weak, and the poor. Jesus loved all people equally, young and old, rich and poor, educated and ignorant, dirty and clean, weak and powerful. Try picturing Jesus gently taking the babies and small children into His arms and looking into their little faces with adoring love. His disciples, Mark and Matthew, also wrote about this scene in their gospel accounts. Mark added this description: "***And He took them up in His arms, laid His hands on them, and blessed them*** *(Mark 10:16).*

That shows the affection that Jesus had for the littlest people, **babies**. And yet in our world today babies are the targets of the worst crimes of all because they can't fight back. Their lives are being snuffed out while they are still in their mothers' wombs, before they even see the light of day. The laws of our nation do not protect them in a lot of places. Some mothers think they must get an abortion (killing a baby in the womb) because if they let the baby be born, it will make problems in their lives. Maybe the mother is not married and is too young to care for it and doesn't have a job or money to support this little life. She is scared, and people around her are telling her an abortion is the answer. No one has to know, they think.

Sadly, many of these girls and women have never put their trust in Jesus, and they believe the devil's lies coming out of the mouths of people close to them. Jesus is the answer. He will provide **a way** for the confused mother and prevent the murder of an innocent baby. One solution is for the baby to be born and given to a married couple who are unable to have children of their own. They can **adopt** this unwanted child. Jesus will not only **show** the way, He **IS** the Way. He said, "I am the Way, the Truth, and the Life" (John 14:6). Jesus loves babies, and He loves their mothers. He wants LIFE for them!

One outstanding example of a famous person who would not be alive today if his mother had listened to the doctors advising her to have an abortion. They said she might die giving birth. She made the decision to trust God with her life, whether she survived childbirth or died. Her faith in God paid off. Tim Tebow was born, and he has made a big impact on our world today, not only in sports, but in his good works, benefiting needy people. Another thing to consider is God may be sending us a cure for cancer, but what if the person He will use to discover the cure is killed in an abortion?

The Lord God created us. He has great plans for each of us. <u>Say this out loud</u> with the Psalmist: *"For You formed my inward parts; You knit me together in my mother's womb. I will praise You, for I am fearfully and wonderfully made; marvelous are Your works, and that my soul knows very well…. Your eyes saw my substance, being yet unformed. And in Your book they all were written, the days fashioned for me, when as yet there were none of them" (Psalm 139:13-16).* Wow! God sees ahead and knows every detail of our lives, day by day. Just like He made the first man Adam from the ground, He forms our little bodies before we are born! Jesus loves us even in the womb.

PRAYER: Thank You, Lord, for creating me. Never let me forget that I am the work of Your hands. Help me to respect every person and not look down on anyone who is different from me, because You created us all and have a plan for each life. In Jesus' name. Amen.

QUESTIONS: What did the disciples do when people brought their babies (infants) and little children to Jesus so He could bless them? How did God create Adam, the first man? (Read Genesis 2:7.) How did God create you and me, and in what **place** did He create us?

14. The Boy King

*"When Athaliah, the mother of King Ahaziah of Judah, learned that her son was dead, she began to destroy the rest of Judah's royal family. But Ahaziah's sister Jehosheba, the daughter of King Jehoram, took Ahaziah's **infant son, Joash**, and stole him away from among the rest of the king's children, who were about to be killed. She put Joash and his nurse in a bedroom. In this way, Jehosheba, wife of Jehoiada the priest and sister of Ahaziah, hid the child so that Athaliah could not murder him. **Joash remained hidden in the Temple of God for six years** while Athaliah ruled over the land"* (2 Chron. 22:10-12, NLT).

Saul, the first king of Israel, was crowned king a thousand years before Jesus was born. David became king after him, and then his son Solomon was king. It was a time of peace for long years until Solomon's son Rehoboam was king. He treated the people so bad they almost had a civil war, and the land of Israel divided into a northern kingdom named Israel and a southern kingdom named Judah. Both kingdoms had twenty kings each over hundreds of years. A seven-year-old boy named Joash became the 8th king in Judah. All the 20 northern kings were wicked, and only eight of the 20 southern kings were good! God had made a covenant with King David. God said, "Your house and your kingdom will continue before Me for all time, and your throne will be secure forever" (2 Samuel 7:16). God had to make sure His promise was carried out, and one day Jesus, who was called the Son of David, would sit on that throne forever! Jesus was a descendant of Joash, so God made sure Joash would become King of Judah.

The angel Gabriel appeared to Jesus' mother before He was born and gave her some shocking news! *"Do not be afraid, Mary, for you have found favor with God. And behold, you will conceive in your womb and bring forth a Son and shall call His name* Jesus. *He will be great and will be called the Son of the Highest; and* **the Lord God will give Him the throne of**

His father David. _And He will reign over the house of Jacob [Israel] forever, and_ **_of His kingdom there will be no end_**" (Luke 1:30-33).

(Read the beginning Scripture again.) The life of the boy king Joash had to be saved, so God's promise could be fulfilled. His wicked grandmother, Athaliah, had been ruling as a queen until the real boy king was brought out of hiding and crowned King of Judah. Jehoida, the Priest, put his plan into action, bringing out the captains, their guards, and runners and giving them spears and shields. Then they formed a ring all around King Joash and put the royal crown on his head. They put a copy of the law in his hands by which to rule, clapped their hands, and shouted, "Long live the king!" Athaliah was taken away and killed, and the people rejoiced. Jehoiada was the young king's advisor and teacher, and King Joash learned how to rule wisely. He did what was right. During his time on the throne, he repaired the temple, which was his greatest achievement. It was in terrible condition due to Athaliah's plundering it for the worship of Baal, the main idol in those days.

Imagine your own grandmother trying to kill you! Some people will do anything to get what they want. Athaliah wanted the throne of Judah for her own selfish reasons. In contrast, looking at the life of Joash, we can see unselfish behavior. He listened to and followed the advice of Jehoida, the Priest, and did what was right for the people he was ruling. He took on the hard job of getting the temple back in good condition after things in it were used for idol worship. Remember when you have a hard job to do, and you are too young to know how to do it, that you need to follow the instructions of someone older and wiser to help you get it done.

PRAYER: Dear Heavenly Father, give me a servant's heart in doing work for the good of others. Don't let me be too proud to ask for help from someone who knows more about it than I do. In Jesus' name. Amen.

QUESTION: When Solomon became King of Israel, God gave Solomon the opportunity to ask for anything he wanted. What did he ask for, and what did God give him? (Read 1 Kings 3:7-14.)

15. The King Who Got Rid of Idols

"Josiah was eight years old when he became king [Joash was 6], and he reigned thirty-one years in Jerusalem. And he did what was right in the sight of the Lord and walked in the ways of his father David; he did not turn aside to the right hand or to the left. For in the eighth year of his reign, while he was still young, he began to seek the God of his father [ancestor] David; and in the twelfth year he began to purge Judah and Jerusalem of the high places, the wooden images, the carved images, and the molded images [idols]" (2 Chron. 34: 1-3).

King Josiah was the 16th king of Judah, coming after King Joash about 200 years later, and they both were boy kings. The Bible doesn't say what Josiah's life was like as an eight-year-old when he became king, but it does say he was 16 years old when he began to serve the Lord. The Lord was going to use him to do great things. Idols were everywhere in Israel. By the time Josiah was 20, he had rid the whole land of idols!

When God first rescued his chosen people from slavery in Egypt, He had Moses lead them to Mt. Sinai where He gave them His laws to live by. There were hundreds of laws, and Moses wrote them in a book, instructions for being healthy, having good relationships in the family and with others, worshiping God with sacrifices, keeping the camp clean, and everything you can think of. Moses went up on the mountain to get the first ten laws, the most important ones, and God wrote them with His finger on two stone tablets. We call them the Ten Commandments. The very first one was: "You shall have no other gods before Me" (Ex. 20:3). The second one was, "You shall not make for yourself a carved image...." (Ex. 20:4). The people broke the first and second commandments right away when they made a statue of a golden calf and bowed down to worship it!

These images, so-called gods, are what we call idols [statues of wood, stone, or metal, and poles]. In King Josiah's day they covered the land! After all the miracles the real God had performed for them, can you believe they did this? God had to judge them over and over, but by the year 586 B.C., God finally did what the prophets had been warning about over many years. God let the Babylonians conquer them, burn down the temple, and take the people captive to Babylon. They stayed there 70 years until they repented of idolatry. After God brought them back to Jerusalem to rebuild the temple, they never worshiped idols again. It's too bad it took such a harsh judgment to cure them of idolatry.

Both young kings, Joash and Josiah, got rid of idols in Israel and repaired the temple. In King Josiah's day during the temple repair, Hilkiah the priest found the book of the Law of God that had been thrown aside. He took it to the king. When Josiah read it, he was so upset he cried and tore his clothes! The people had broken all the laws of God in the book, and God had said He would destroy the land! Josiah brought all the people to the temple, and he read the entire Book of the Covenant to them and made them promise to keep God's law. They made a covenant with God there. "All his days they did not depart from following the Lord God of their fathers" (2 Chron. 34:33). Sad to say, this wasn't true of King Joash who turned to idolatry at the end of his life! King Josiah was the last good king of Judah. Four bad kings followed him, and then Jerusalem was destroyed and the people taken captive.

Josiah's grandfather, King Manasseh, had placed idols everywhere. He worshiped the stars and even put idols in the temple! He murdered the prophet Isaiah. Worst of all, he sacrificed his own son in the fire! He was the wickedest of all 20 kings of Judah, and he reigned the longest – 55 years! He led the whole nation in worshiping idols. His son Amon reigned two years, and he was wicked, too. Josiah had a terrible family history, but it didn't stop him from being a good king. Some Bible scholars think that Josiah was the second-best king of Judah after King David, and he started ruling at only eight years old! Don't let your age or your family history stop you from doing great things for God.

PRAYER: Dear Lord, thank you for showing me that being a child doesn't keep me from carrying out some important work for You. Josiah didn't "turn aside to the right hand or to the left." He was only eight, and he walked straight ahead on the "paths of righteousness" you laid out before him. I want to do the same. Help me. In Jesus' name. Amen.

QUESTIONS: What book did the priest find in the temple that upset King Josiah? What did he do after he read it?

16. Keep Yourselves from Idols

"Little children, keep yourselves from idols. Amen." (1 John 5:21).

You may think, "I would never have worshiped idols! Anyway, we don't have idols today." But wait, stop, and think. What is it in your life that you spend most of your time on and your money and also your affections? That thing may be an idol in your life, something that you love more than God. An idol can be money or beauty pageants or sports or being popular. You can even make an idol out of yourself! Do you think about yourself all the time and what you want instead of what God wants? When you break this first commandment, you break God's heart. God doesn't need anything, but He does want your love and your worship. He wants to shower you with His blessings, but when you commit idolatry, you cut yourself off from His blessings.

The Apostle John adored Jesus. He knew Jesus loved him, and that caused John to stay as close to Him as he could. John is called "the disciple Jesus loved" (John 13:23). He wrote the Gospel of John and three letters in the Bible. The very last verse in John's first letter is 5:21. It sums up the most important thing in the letter – "Little children, keep yourselves from idols. Amen." He knew that would keep us from loving God, which is His first commandment. Remember, the Jewish people didn't worship idols anymore after they came back from Babylon in 537 B.C., so John wasn't talking about carved images, stone statues, or metal statues. He was talking about the things in our lives that are more valuable to us than our Heavenly Father and Jesus.

The story Jesus told about the rich young ruler proves you can't serve Jesus and an idol at the same time. You have to choose between them. This young man approached Jesus with a question. He wanted to know what he had to do to have eternal life (never die), and Jesus asked **him** questions about how he had obeyed God's laws. The young man said he obeyed them all since he was a child! But he didn't understand that obeying the first four of the Ten Commandments meant you loved God, and obeying the last six commandments proved that you loved others. Actually, all the laws were about love, not about keeping a list of rules. "**Jesus looked at him and loved him**. 'One thing you lack,' He said. 'Go, sell everything you have and give to the poor, and you will have treasure in heaven. Then come, follow me.' At this the man's face fell. He went away sad, because he had great wealth" (Mark 10:21-22, NIV).

John said, "Loving God means keeping his commandments, and his commandments are not burdensome" (1 John 5:3, NLT). It's easy to obey

someone you love. The rich young ruler loved his possessions, things money could buy, more than He loved Jesus. He didn't respond to Jesus' love like John did, and he missed out on being one of Jesus' first disciples! He missed out on seeing Jesus up close, doing miracles, healing blind eyes and deaf ears, and walking on water. Picture this: a hungry dog is gnawing on an old bone. You come toward him with a piece of juicy steak. The dog thinks you are trying to take his bone away from him, so he holds on tighter to the bone and won't drop it and take the juicy steak! That's what the rich young ruler did. Loving his idol, which was money, cut off the blessings from God he could have had.

PRAYER: Dear Jesus, I know I can depend on You to give me everything I need in this life, so I promise not to have any idols. You are real, and they are just things. Knowing that You love me is the greatest reason to get rid of idols in my heart. Help me keep this promise. I love You.

QUESTIONS: What did the Apostle John mean when he said God's laws are not burdensome? When you love someone and they tell you to do something, what do you do, and how does it make you feel? Or what did you fail to do, and how did that make you feel?

17. Go into Your World

"Go therefore and make disciples [followers of Jesus] of all the nations, baptizing them in the name of the Father and of the Son and of the Holy Spirit, teaching them to observe all things that I have commanded you; and lo, I am with you always, even to the end of the age. Amen" (Matthew 28:19-20).

Have you thought about what kind of job you want when you finish your education and go out in the world, get married, and have children? Do you think you should pick the job that pays the highest salary? But does that job match your abilities? Why not think about what God has planned for you to do? He has a plan for you, your family, and your job. Your life's work will fit in with the gifts and talents He created you with. It will be the kind of work you will enjoy and can be good at. When you asked Jesus to save you, He made you a citizen of His kingdom on earth, and your primary job is to grow His kingdom by winning more people to believe in Jesus. That starts now, not when you are getting a paycheck at some job.

The last instruction Jesus gave His disciples before He went back to heaven was to **make disciples** of all nations [all over the world] and to teach these new disciples everything Jesus had taught them. He promised to **be with** His disciples to give them power to do this. You may be thinking, "I don't want to be a missionary." In Mark's gospel it says, "Go into **all the world** and preach the gospel to all creation" (Mark 16:15, NIV). All Christians should be missionaries. We can go into **OUR world**, where we live and work, and win people to Jesus. Paul was a full-time missionary, but he still had to have a job to make money to support himself. He made tents in the different places God sent him so he could do his first job, making disciples.

Think about the thing that is easy for you to do, something that brings you joy, and other people have told you that you are good at doing that.

They say that you have a talent for it. These are God's clues that will help you choose a job or career. A little girl might gather her stuffed animals and dolls, arrange them in rows, stand up in front of them, and pretend they are in a classroom. This shows that God probably created her with the gift of teaching. What do you think God created **you** to do? He wants you to win people to Jesus while you are doing this job. Here's another example: you see a boy setting up a stand to sell lemonade in his front yard on a hot day. He enjoys making advertising signs and placing them around town, and he is really good at counting the money and buying more supplies. Does God plan for him to be a businessman? Or have you noticed the person that steps up to keep order in the classroom when the teacher suddenly leaves? The students are willing to listen and follow that person's directions. God will use those leadership qualities in the life work of that person.

Your "world" right now is school, church, friends, and your family, including those who don't live in your house. If you are on a sports team or in some other group, like a club, a band, or with girls in a beauty pageant, that is also your world. We are all preachers. The word "preach" means "proclaim" or speak out about the good news that Jesus died to save us from our sins and give us everlasting life in heaven with Him and the Heavenly Father. So these are some of the places you can "make disciples" for Jesus. For instance, if He answered a prayer for you that was amazing, you should tell it to your world! Others may want to know more about following Jesus. Or you could ask people in your world what they need prayer for. You could even pray for that request right then if it's possible to get alone with that person. Nothing will give you more joy than helping someone to get to know Jesus. Some time when you are having spend-the-night company, you could ask that friend to join you and your parent in reading a devotional from this book. It is exciting when something like that happens, and you can feel the Holy Spirit has planned it way ahead of time, because He has been drawing that child to Himself. He wants you to be a part of a changed life! Obey Him when the Spirit is nudging you.

PRAYER: Dear Jesus, thank You for giving me an important job of being used to change lives! Help me to realize that You have put me where I am because You need me to make disciples in my world. I know I may seem strange to the people around me at times, but help me to want Your approval more than theirs.

QUESTIONS: Do you know where your "world" is, and who is in it that you feel the Holy Spirit wants you to make a disciple of Jesus? How would you go about doing it? Is the best reason for choosing a job or profession the amount of money you will get paid?

18. Life!

"The thief does not come except to steal, and to kill, and to destroy. I have come that they may have LIFE, and that they may have it more abundantly" (John 10:10).

Our God created all life upon the earth. First, He prepared the earth out of nothing to be a home for His final and best creations, man and woman. "For we are God's handiwork, created in Christ Jesus to do good works, which God prepared in advance for us to do" (Eph. 2:10, NIV). God formed Adam out of dirt with His own hands. Then He blew into his nostrils the breath of life, and man became a living being (Gen. 2:7). Everything was perfect until Adam and Eve sinned. They brought death into the world. But God already had a plan. "God so loved the world that He gave His only begotten Son [Jesus], that whosoever believes in Him should not perish but have everlasting life" (John 3:16). Jesus was the sacrifice for our sins – past, present, and future!

Thousands of years later when Jesus walked the earth, He taught the people that He came to give them life, the kind of life He called "abundant," meaning plenty of it, large amounts, a life where your needs and desires are met. He even called Himself LIFE! He explained how to get to heaven: "I am the Way, the Truth, and the Life. No one comes to the Father except by Me" (John 14:6). He doesn't just **show** us the way to heaven. He IS the way. He doesn't just give us abundant life. He IS life!

You are reading the 18th devotional in this book right now. In the Hebrew language 18 stands for "life," according to the number given to each letter of the Hebrew alphabet. The Hebrew word for life is ***chai***. The plural form is ***chaim*** and is pronounced "hi-yeem." ***L'chaim*** (Luh hiyeem) means "to life," and is a kind of congratulations. Jesus is Jewish, and He spoke Hebrew. He probably toasted the couple at the wedding feast in Cana of Galilee after He performed His first miracle of turning the water into wine. In your imagination, picture Him raising His glass of wine to the couple and saying, "L'Chaim!" (Story in John 2:1-11).

Your parents have the job of raising you to live the life God has **called you** to live. What the Apostle Paul taught his student Timothy is exciting: "*God has saved us and **called us** with a holy calling, not according to our works, but according to **His own purpose and grace which was given to us in Christ Jesus before time began**" (2 Tim. 1:9).* Just think, He planned your life BEFORE TIME BEGAN! God will show your parents how to raise you: "*Train up a child in the way he should go [teaching him to seek God's wisdom and will for **his abilities and talents**]. Even when he is old he will not depart from it" (Prov. 22:6, Amplified Bible).*

Your parents may have heard this saying, "As the twig is bent, so grows the tree." That means that the influences in **your life as a child** will have a permanent effect. Parents are so blessed that they can work with God in molding your life (bending the twig) into the man or woman God wants you to become. Your life is a gift from God. Treat yourself with respect and always be seeking God's will for your life. Don't worry that you won't be able to find out God's will. He wants that more than you do, and He is not trying to hide His will from you. "For **it is God** who works in you both **to will and to do** for His good pleasure" (Phil. 2:13). Jesus will lead you into that life work prepared for you before time began. You know He is your Savior, but be sure He is your **Lord**. Lord means BOSS! When He calls, answer and follow.

PRAYER: Father God, thank You for the abundant life I have with Jesus as my Savior and Lord. I know I will never be bored when I let You lead, and I follow. It takes a load off my shoulders when You are the boss. May Your will (not my will) be done and Your kingdom come on earth as it is in heaven. In Jesus' name I pray. Amen.

QUESTIONS: Is there another way to get to heaven besides believing Jesus died for our sins on the cross and receiving His forgiveness? What kind of life did Jesus come to give us? What does Chai mean, and what is the number for it in Hebrew? If Jesus raised His glass and toasted the newlyweds when he performed His first miracle at Cana of Galilee, what might he have said?

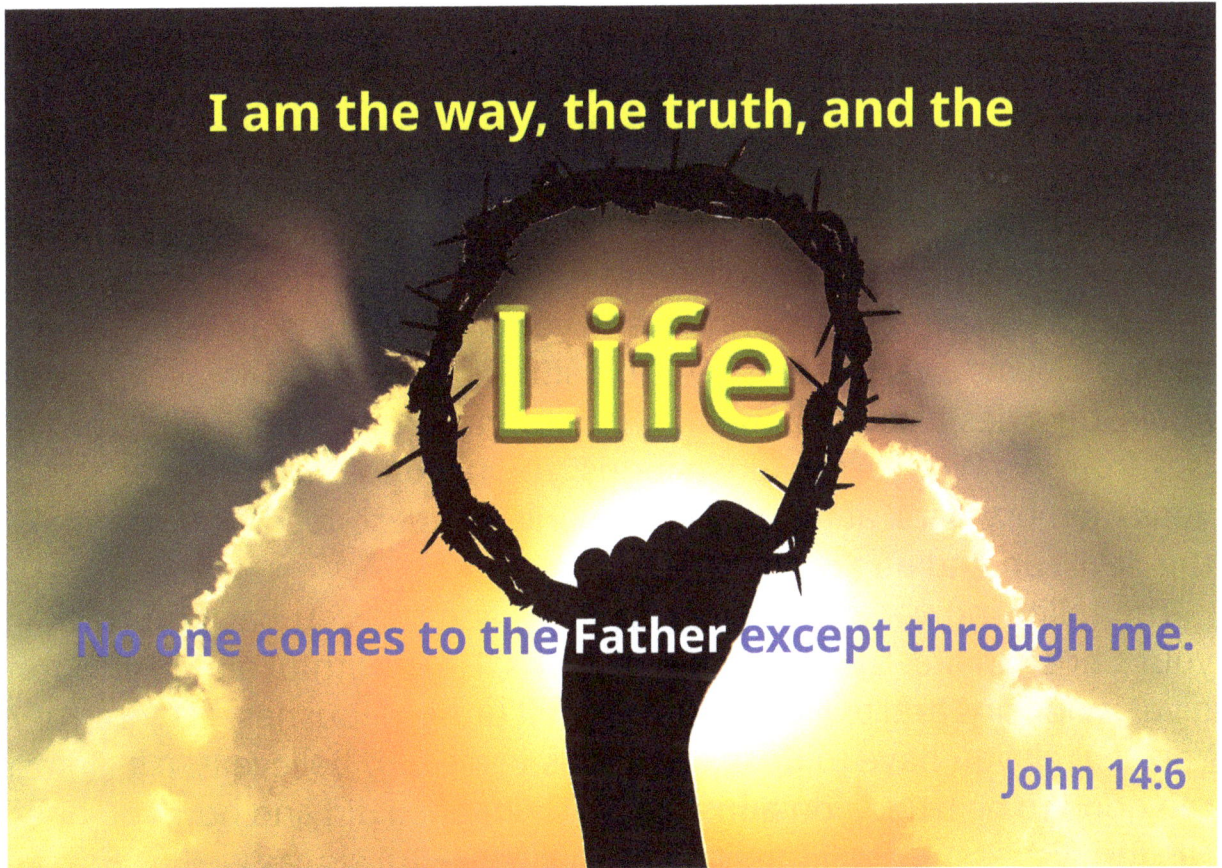

I am the way, the truth, and the Life

No one comes to the Father except through me.

John 14:6

Living The Christian Life

The very first sin committed on earth was Adam and Eve's disobeying God, and it brought death into the world. These devotionals were written to help children to obey God. In obeying your parents, you are obeying God. Honoring your parents is the first commandment with a promise: that it may be well with you, and that you may live long on the earth (Eph. 6:1-3). When you accepted Jesus Christ as your Savior and Lord, you were forgiven all your sins and you were given everlasting life. But what happens **after** that when you sin?

The devil is real, and he is that thief that comes to "steal, kill, and destroy" (John 10:10). You can't see him, but he whispers lies in your ear. You may not be aware that he does this to make you give up on yourself and God and quit following Jesus. You may think it is your own thoughts. Maybe you just sinned, and you think there is no hope for you because it was a very bad sin. For this situation you need some weapons against the lies filling your mind and robbing you of peace. God's promises from His Word are your weapons. You need to have some verses in your memory bank at a time like the one just described. You can make the devil run and quit bothering you.

The following verse will give you hope and get you back on track in your Christian life: "If we **confess** our sins, He is faithful and just to forgive us our sins and to cleanse us from **all** unrighteousness" (1 John 1:9). You see, all you have to do is quote this verse and believe it. It's almost too good to be true – you **admit** to God what you did and how you need His forgiveness. He will forgive you for that awful sin, as well as forgive you (cleanse you) from **all the other sins** you **didn't** confess! How wonderful! It's important that you have this verse memorized, so you can keep it handy when the devil attacks you in your mind. Then you won't be depressed. You will be happy and filled with hope.

Don't let Satan try to convince you that you are not really saved because you sinned. When Jesus was washing the feet of His disciples the night before He was arrested, Peter was amazed that His Master would act like a servant, doing what only servants did. He protested that Jesus would not wash his feet. And Jesus said if Peter wouldn't let Him, he wouldn't belong to Him. Then Peter told the Lord that He could not only wash his feet, but also his hands and head! Jesus said, "A person who has bathed all over (has been saved) does not need to wash, except for the feet, to be entirely clean" (John 13:10, NLT). The meaning of that was we don't have to be saved all over again, if we once accepted Jesus as Lord and Savior. The dirt we get on our feet as we walk through this sinful world is the only thing we need to have cleaned off, the same as confessing our most recent sin to the Lord and having Him say, "You're forgiven." (Story in John 13.) Besides, Jesus died on the cross two thousand years before you were born, and the salvation He purchased for us at that time in history covers our past, present, and future!

Important verses for you to memorize are listed at the end of this book. The Psalmist said, "Your word I have **hidden** in my heart, that I might not sin against You" (Psa. 119:11). **Memorizing** parts of the Bible is like hiding God's Word in your heart to keep you from sinning. Paul said that the Word of God is like a sword of the Spirit. This is part of your armor against the devil who wants to trip you up and cause you to sin. Also, your faith is like a shield to stop the fiery darts of the wicked one (Eph. 6:10-18).

God gave us the Bible as humanity's operating manual. Get familiar with it. It is divided into two parts – Old Covenant and New Covenant.

Jesus is hidden in the Old part, and right out in the open in the New part. There are 66 books – 39 in the Old and 27 in the New – and every book is important. Forty men were used by God to write it, all Jewish except for one, Luke. The Old Covenant was written in Hebrew and the New Covenant was mostly written in Greek. The Holy Spirit showed the writers exactly what to write, and we can be sure every word is true and is sent from God. The Apostle Paul taught his student Timothy, *"**All** Scripture is **inspired by God** and is useful to teach us what is true and to make us realize what is wrong in our lives. It corrects us when we are wrong and teaches us to do what is right. God uses it to prepare and equip his people to do **every good work**" (2 Tim. 3:16-17, NLT).*

There is no way you can have a good life, be happy, and do useful work without knowing the Bible. Some people read it all the way through every year, but God doesn't command us to do it. However, the first sign you are really saved is that you will hunger and thirst for the Word of God. When people all around are believing the lies of the devil and living unhappy, sinful lives, you will know the truth, and God will use you to be a light in the darkness. Pick a place every day, in the morning or at night, where you can get alone with God, read the Bible, and pray. Add singing to your devotional time, and you will have joy. Let the Holy Spirit show you the way He wants you to read your Bible. He may start you out in the New Testament with the four gospels – Matthew, Mark, Luke, and John – for you to get the whole picture of Jesus' life on earth. Don't feel any pressure to keep to a schedule, but make sure you read something every day, even if it is only one Psalm, one chapter in the New Testament, or one chapter in the Old Testament. In your prayer, first thank the Lord for specific things He has done for you and praise Him. That is a good time to sing to Him. In your requests, include our country, the nation of Israel (where Jesus is returning one day), your family, your friends, those you know who need to be saved, and those you know who need to be physically healed or comforted. Don't pray for people in general, like "those who are sick," but call out names of people you know. The Holy Spirit will bring people to your mind, if you wait on Him. Pray for yourself, too.

Ask the Holy Spirit to help you pray. Every Christian needs to be filled with the Spirit. He is God's best gift. Without Him, you won't have any **power** to carry out God's plan for your life. All you have to do is ASK! "So I say to you, ask, and it will be given to you; seek, and you will find; knock, and it will be opened to you. For everyone who asks receives, and he who seeks finds, and to him who knocks it will be opened. If a son asks for bread from any father among you, will he give him a stone? Or if he asks for a fish, will he give him a serpent instead of a fish? Or if he asks for an egg, will he offer him a scorpion? If you then, being evil, know how to give good gifts to your children, how much more will your heavenly Father give the Holy Spirit to those who ask Him!" (Luke 11:9-13).

FINAL WORD TO PARENTS: Train up your child in the way he/she should go (Prov. 22:6). In Hebrew the word isn't "train." It is "narrow." Narrow means "guide, directing to a certain way." A child can go in any direction. Your responsibility is to "narrow them to the Word, narrow them to God's way, to righteousness. Narrow them to be godly people, to be giving people. Narrow their ways. Guard them from evil influences."[1] Parents, narrow your own way because "strait is the gate, and narrow is the way, which leadeth unto life, and few there be that find it" (Matt. 7:14, KJV). Jesus said that.

---

1   Jonathan Cahn, *Sapphires* devotional booklet, Hope of the World: Lodi, NJ, August 23, 2023.

Memory Verses

1. "Children, obey your parents in the Lord, for this is right. 'Honor your father and mother,' which is the first commandment with promise: 'that it may be well with you and you may live long on the earth'" (Ephesians 6:1-3).

2. "Then He went down with them and came to Nazareth, and was **obedient** to them, but His mother kept all these things in her heart. And Jesus increased in wisdom and stature, and in favor with God and men" (Luke 2:51-52).

3. "Enter into His gates with thanksgiving, and into His courts with praise. Be thankful unto Him and bless His name. For the Lord is good; His mercy is everlasting, and His truth endures to all generations" (Psalm 100:4-5).

4. "The next day John saw Jesus coming toward him, and said, 'Behold! The Lamb of God who takes away the sin of the world!'" (John 1:29).

5. "For unto us a Child is born, unto us a Son is given; and the government will be upon His shoulder. And His name will be called Wonderful, Counselor, Mighty God, Everlasting Father, Prince of Peace" (Isaiah 9:6).

6. "For God so loved the world that He gave His only begotten Son, that whoever believes in Him should not perish but have everlasting life" (John 3:16).

7. "...You must all be quick to listen, slow to speak, and slow to get angry. Human anger does not produce the righteousness God desires" (James 1:19-20,NIV).

8. "... the Lord does not see as man sees; for man looks at the outward appearance, but the Lord looks at the heart" (1 Samuel 16:7).

9. "But Jesus called them to Him and said, 'Let the little children come to Me, and do not forbid them; for of such is the kingdom of God. Assuredly, I say to you, whoever does not receive the kingdom of God as a little child will by no means enter it'" (Luke 18:16-17).

10. "For You formed my inward parts; You covered me in my mother's womb. I will praise You, for I am fearfully and wonderfully made; marvelous are Your works, and that my soul knows very well" (Psalm 139:13-14).

11. "Little children, keep yourselves from idols. Amen." (1 John 5:21).

12. "For this is the love of God, that we keep His commandments. And His commandments are not burdensome" (1John 5:3).

13. "Go into all the world and preach the gospel to all creation" (Mark 16:15, NIV).

14. "The thief does not come except to steal, and to kill, and to destroy. I have come that they may have life, and that they may have it more abundantly" (John 10:10).

15. "For we are God's handiwork, created in Christ Jesus to do good works, which God prepared in advance for us to do" (Eph. 2:10, NIV).

16. "If we confess our sins, He is faithful and just to forgive us our sins and to cleanse us from all unrighteousness" (1John 1:9).

17. "Jesus said to him, 'I am the Way, the Truth, and the Life. No one comes to the Father except through Me'" (John 14:6).

18. "All Scripture is inspired by God and is useful to teach us what is true and to make us realize what is wrong in our lives. It corrects us when we are wrong and teaches us to do what is right. God uses it to prepare and equip His people to do every good work" (2 Tim. 3:16-17, NLT).

More Devotionals by Nancy Petrey

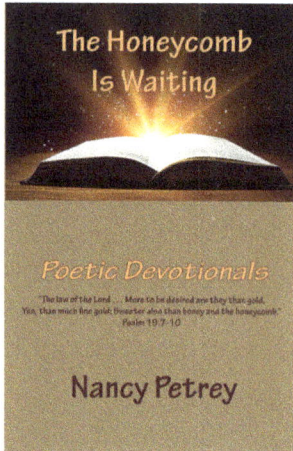

The Honeycomb Is Waiting: Poetic Devotionals

https://www.energiondirect.com/product/the-honeycomb-is-waiting-direct

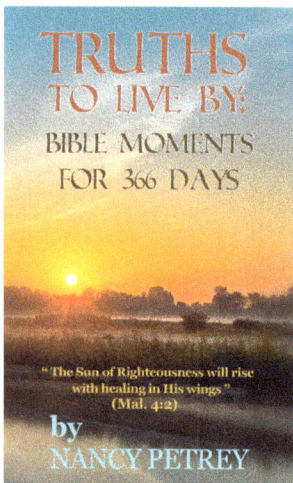

For Amazon Kindle: *Truths to Live By*
https://amzn.to/2J5AI3B

See all of Nancy Petrey's ten books:

https://www.energiondirect.com/product-category/authors/nancy-petrey/

www.ingramcontent.com/pod-product-compliance
Lightning Source LLC
Chambersburg PA
CBHW062054090426
42740CB00016B/3131